The Diary of She

Vol II: Poems and Affirmations

Sydney Reneé

The Diary of She 2

ISBN: 979-8-9859044-2-0

United States:
10 9 8 7 6 5 4 3 2

The Diary of She
2

DEAR, DIARY

It's me again!

Still making mistakes but growing from them. I've come to realize that not everyone is as caring as they should be, nor do we share the same emotional maturity. People have continued to question my loyalty and have tried to depict me as the enemy. I'm at the point where I no longer ponder on who wants the best for me or who is truly in my corner. The screaming and shouting as stopped and the threatening messages have come to a halt. *Shame on me for letting so many bring out the worst in me.*

I've learned to be straightforward with my feelings, telling myself that if they aren't reciprocated it's fine to drift away peaceful. There's no need for me to make a scene on my way out. I know something healthier on the other side is waiting for me, something that makes sense...

A life worth going through, the nights spent alone.

A life worth going through, the people who have come and gone.

A life that tells me there's someone out there for me that's sincere.

A life that I created after getting rid of all the negative energy.

A life that will teach me a lot and bless me with a lot more.

xoxo
SHE

THE BAD

Comes before the good

OPEN BOOK

Before she handed over the story of her life, she
ripped out every page that held the secrets she
wanted to keep stored away.

She placed them in a file and vowed to never show
a soul until, one day, she was no longer ashamed.
She took those pages filled with secrets and let
them fly.

TAKING CONTROL

Vulnerable.
Fragile.
Taken advantage of.
Losing hope.

This is what life had become.

Afraid and weak.
That's not who she was.

He came along pretending to be a friend.
Making her comfortable.
Breaking down every barrier.
Motives behind every little thing.

At her lowest, he saw his chance.
He took it, and he failed.
It still broke her.

Losing control.
Being extremely reckless.
Acting out of character.

That is what life had become.

Giving away what was so precious.
Sacred parts of her that should have been saved.
Thinking why hold on if they'll take it away.

Forcing themselves through.
Breaking down the entryway.

Sydney Reneé

Ignoring the screams.
Continuing anyway.

She was losing it.
She thought it was the only way.
She thought she had taken control.
She hadn't found her way.

HELP-HER

I was depressed, but I refused to tell anyone.
No one would notice my disappearance.
Currently no one acknowledged my existence.

BACK TO YOU

I found her,
no longer missing.
roaming around in the rain.

So cold, delicate, and lonely.

I swooped her off her feet and carried her home,
placed her in a warm bath and washed away the
hurt.

I could see she was drifting.
Soon she would be gone.

Please, stay.
I need you.
With me, you're safe.

As she sank to the bottom, she seen a light.
Visioning paradise, ready for a new life.

Don't go.
It'll be okay.
Don't go.
There will be better days.

Closing her eyes, she was ready to say goodbye.
She no longer wanted to live a terrible life but
She heard a voice screaming, *"This isn't right."*

Come back.
It's not your time.

Give life another try.

SUICIDE

I couldn't do it.
I was too afraid to take my life.
Instead, I went running back to him.
With him, I didn't feel alive.
I felt a void I didn't want filled.
I felt useless and nonexistent.
With him, I suffered.
He was my way out.
The closest I could get to death.

WELCOME HOME

The longer it took me to arrive at his house, I wondered if God was trying to give me time to think about my decision, giving me a way out.

I had been ignoring him for months, so I could get my feelings in check.

I circled the block twice before finally parking my car. As I approached the front door, as always, he had it unlocked for me. I entered his room, and he welcomed me with open arms.

"You finally decided to come home," he said as I settled into his arms.

ALARMS

Every morning, she anticipated waking up to his name on her phone screen. From 5-8 p.m., she watched the clock hoping for it to ring.

Every night before she fell asleep, she prayed he was okay and that just maybe he was thinking the same.

THE WAITING GAME

I would look at him and ask myself why I wasn't
enough.
I would look at him and think of all the ways I
could get him to stay.

I spent so much time trying to figure out *why them?*
Wondering when he'd see I was the one
Wasting time on a man who can't love me.

Now, I look at him, waiting for him to leave.
So, I could silently set myself free.

SIDE EFFECTS

I wanted to be the one who helped him become a
better man.
He was only making me a worse woman.

PARTNERS

She didn't want to be saved.
She wanted you in her corner.
Even Wonder Woman needed back up at times.

OPTIONS...

I remember the day he cried for me.
That day, I felt special, like we had a bond so
strong it couldn't be broken.

Then, I watched him fall to his knees begging the
next woman and the one after her not to leave.

I was just one of his options...

WHEN OPPOSITES ATTRACT

From the beginning, I knew he was wrong for me.
The two of us didn't mix like oil and water.
I disregarded my feelings until I couldn't anymore.
Part of me wishes I left him where we met.
That when he got out my car, I never looked back.
It wouldn't have taken us on a journey of love and regrets.

NO LOVE ALLOWED

Caught in euphoria.
Unable to break free from the intensity in his eyes.
A forbidden romance wasn't what she was after.
An unlikely encounter, too late to turn away.
She knew it would end in disaster.

DESTRUCTION AHEAD

How can you look me in the eyes and say I've
never been there for you? Looking back at you, I
can see our whole journey playing on a loop.

Who was there giving you a shoulder to cry on
when the world made you feel like you had to walk
around in permanent armor?

The world made you feel like you had to remain
hard to receive respect, but I assured you your
emotions only added to the strength you possessed,
and if you felt the need to hide from the world, you
didn't have to hide yourself from me.

You let your emotions flow like a river, and I was
there to float freely with you.

My dear, please, don't act like I wasn't there
helping you, building you up when you were at
your lowest with no one around to lift your spirits
to heights higher than the highest.

Treating you like the light that guided my way
through the darkness you were living in when I was
really your sun in the night sky keeping a glow on
your face.

Helping you evolve into the man she sees standing
before her, a man who found his way when he got
lost in the wind and led into a direction that only
read *destruction ahead.*

I traveled long and far to bring you back from the depths of hell only for you to up and leave me to fight the demons of *your* world alone.

ROSE PETALS

He planted the seed.
Watered me daily.
I bloomed beautifully.
The nurturing faded.
Communication ended.
Petals fell until nothing was left.

SHE'S EVERYTHING

The first time he saw her, she hadn't once noticed him.

Eventually he caught her attention.

He was no longer just another face in the crowd but headlining the show.
He kept her laughing and managed to get her out of her comfort zone.

The Weekends turned into a permanent stay.
Trips to the market turned into trips out of town.

I like you turned into *I love you*, which turned into *I can't live without you.*

He was planning their future, but he wasn't prepared for the day he had to say goodbye.

Nowadays, when a woman says, *"hello,"* all he hears is her cries.

CUT HER LOOSE

Beautiful man, she doesn't deserve you.

You provide her with more than she can handle.
She asked for a purse.
You gave her Heaven on Earth,
then came back with the whole fucking universe.
Dedicated to an un-loyal bitch focusing on the
next,
but a "bitch" is something you'd never call her.
Even with all the disrespect she presents you with,
you love her, but she doesn't like you.
She needs you, but she doesn't want you.
They'll never treat her the way you do.

Beautiful man, cut that woman loose.

PICTURE PERFECT

Cut up pictures on my bedroom floor,
Removing every trace of you I could.
Sadly, memories of you remained.

WITH THIS RING

Promise rings came with broken promises.
I know from experience...

I can remember the first time I received my own:

It was gold with about four small diamonds lined in
a row.
The thought behind it was so beautiful.
Though the smile on my face didn't last long.

With this ring came a double life, full of betrayal
and lies.
It was another woman's ring, one that always came
before me.

I remember losing that ring, and a relief it was.

FINDERS KEEPERS

He was a chance at love,
a chance she shouldn't have taken.
All he did was take her for granted.
Granting all his wishes yet
wishing for the same in return.
A keeper, he wasn't.

CLUELESS

He knew exactly how to handle my body.
When it came to my heart, he hadn't a fucking
clue.

INCAPABLE

I wondered if he could love me the way I loved
him.
I needed him to change, but I couldn't force him.
I had no control over the way his heart functioned.

I wasn't sure why I stayed.
Perhaps, I thought the change would come one
day.
Either he'd return the love, or he'd escape.

I got used to him leaving, anyway.

WRITINGS ON THE WALL

I was willing to be his punching bag when he came home feeling like everyone was against him. If he wasn't physically putting his hands on me, I felt safe.

What was that saying growing up? *Sticks and stones may break my bones, but words will never hurt me.*

I believed those words and stuck to them, but one day I felt different. Every nasty word he ever said were staring back at me: *worthless, stupid, ugly, slut, waste of space, failure…*

Those words had taken over and I believed that's who I had become.

It was going to take some time to dig through all that filth and find myself again.

STREETWALKER

She stood in the middle of the road looking up at
the stars; Muting the sound of cars honking as they
swerved to avoid clashing into her.

She ignored the little boy across the street pointing.

She tuned out the sounds of dogs barking, couples
fighting and the homeless woman begging.

She let the wind blow viciously across her face.

She was still while everything around her
continued moving.

Dropping to her knees in the middle of all the
catastrophe, she felt everything that was burdening
her leave.

She was happy.

She was at peace.

She felt at home in the middle of that street, but
she knew she couldn't stay there. She knew she
would eventually have to face every problem in her
world.

ALL THE IFs

What if I walked away and returned to you in a
new life?

Would you recognize my eyes and the glow of my
delicate skin?

Would you take one look at me and give me a
chance to love you again?

Would you stare at my lips and imagine how sweet
my kisses taste?

Would you remember the way I'd quiver and shake
when my legs were wrapped around your waist?

Would you wrap me in your warm embrace and
tell me I'm good?

What if I came back to you in a new life?
Would you still be honored to make me your wife?

Would you enjoy lying next to me every night?
Or would you look at me and wish me out of sight?

AGAIN

It was him again.
I envisioned this day for years.
Him and I face-to-face.

What would it look like?
Would we speak?
Would we walk past each other like strangers do on
the street?

It was him again.
I started to feel like the day would never come.
Him and I wrapped in each other becoming one.

I felt frozen, but my body was warm.
My heart was beating like a drum. *Ba-boom. Ba-boom. Ba-boom.*
It went on and on.
Finally, jumping out my chest to see how it felt to
beat next to his once more.

Holding back my tears, he took me in his arms,
embracing me like he had many times before.
Filled with joy but dreading this moment's end.

Slipping from one another but returning for more,
we knew it would be forever before we had this
moment once again.

It was him again…
my dear old friend.

OH, HOW THINGS CHANGE

Those who claim they'd never forget you are
usually the first to forget everything about you…

ALL CRIED OUT

I tried to remember the last time I cried, but that
meant I was going to have to think back on the hell
I went through with you by my side…

BROKEN HEARTS NEED TIME TO HEAL

For a few days, I've been feeling lost within myself, not knowing what to say or how to feel.

First, the feeling of loneliness came and sadness shortly after. The biggest part of me was saying, "break down and cry." Still, I couldn't begin to think of what was wrong with me and why it was hitting me at this exact moment.

While I was driving home, a song came on. Within the second line I was wiping tears from my face trying to control my sobbing. That's when it hit me; *my heart was still broken.* I was hurting.

I gained a new love and lost an old one. Instead of dealing with my loss, I let the anger and hurt build inside of me. I began to act as if my old love no longer existed, like he no longer mattered.

I can't seem to move on.
I'm still holding on to what could be.

For days, I've been trying to figure out what's missing. I'm finally admitting it's my fault that my heart hasn't taken the time it's been needing to recover from the devastation of losing what I thought was a lifetime filled with him.

TAKE A CHANCE

On Love

ONE DAY

One day, I'll write about a love that climbs mountains, travels state-to-state, and crosses the sea looking for me.

I'll write about a love that doesn't quite have a beginning or an ending; we just somehow came to be, and everything worked out perfectly.

One day, I'll write about a love that didn't come and rescue me from the demons I was fighting. Nope, this love will stand by me like a Queen does her King, and we'll fight every battle together.

I'll write about a love that lifts me above the heavens, taking me to dimensions unknown to those who remain lost in the clouds.

One day, I'll write about a love that's better than your favorite love song. A love that I can keep on repeat for an eternity.

THE KEY

You want to turn me on?
Well, take a route you aren't used to.

Study me.
Teach me.
Uplift me.
Empower me.

Look beyond what you see on the outside. Dig way
down into my soul. Ask me about my day and
don't settle for a simple, "It was okay."

Let's discuss each other's dreams and then come up
with a plan to make them a reality. Let's invest in
one another and never stop evolving.

FAR AWAY

He was the rainbow I could never reach.
The cloud I dreamed of resting my head on.
The mountain I wanted to climb.
The ocean I was too afraid to cross.
No matter how close he appeared,
he would never be in my reach.

NOW, I LAY ME

I prayed for the man of my imaginings.
A man sent down from heaven
with the qualities of a King.
A heart of pure gold
and God standing with him.

BIG CITY DREAMS

Let's meet up.
Learn about one another.
Fall in love during the process.
Learn a little more.
Teach each other.
Work toward building our empire.
Get married.
Start a family.
And never fall out of love.

...AND I HOPE YOU DO

I bet you thought every word on this paper was
inspired by you, but you're not the only one to
penetrate me deep. He reached my core, and
every emotion came flowing out of me, washing
away every trace of you that was left behind.

NO CHOICE

She never took him seriously.
Serious was the one thing he couldn't be.
Every move he made; she took for play.
That was until he kissed her with so much passion.
She had no choice but to go on that date.

NO DOUBT

A year ago, we wouldn't be in this position.
I wouldn't have looked your way for a second.
Thoughts of entertaining you wouldn't have
crossed my mind, not even for a minute.

There wasn't a chance in hell that I was going to
give you the opportunity to waste a minute of my
time.

I would have jumped to conclusions.
I would have judged you based off of my past.
I would have assumed you were no better than the
others.

See, I'd been fucked over so much in the past I
didn't have room for error. It was best I avoided
the situation all together, save the hurt for another.

Here we are now…

Looking at you, I can say I have no doubts.
I'm not looking to sabotage you and me.
This time the timing is right.
I know myself and what I won't deal with.
I'm sure about you.
I'm positive we'll make it through.

NEW BAE

He was my new high.
He had me floating through the room,
praying I'd never come down.

High into the sky and over the moon,
he sent me flying, and I'm not sure what to do
Being wrapped in his arms felt like hugs from the
clouds.

My legs around his waist, we were about to drown.
Covered in love, hoping my heart wouldn't break,
I held on tight until my body started to shake.
I could have sworn I felt tears rolling down my
face.

I just might be falling for my new bae.

BEAUTY & THE BEAST

He gazed at me as if I was the loveliest woman, he ever laid eyes on.

Every day, he discovered a new way to admire my beauty.

It wasn't my external appearance that kept him intrigued, but what he uncovered inside of me.

His hard exterior shattered revealing a softer side, but when we made love, the look in his eyes let me know there was still a beast inside.

TAKING RISKS

For this long, you've waited on me.
For this long, you've held onto possibilities.
For this long, you've stayed by me.
For this long, you've continued to support me.

For years, I made sure to stay away.
For years, I ignored your advances.
For years, I continued to make excuses.
For years, I debated is it "yay" or "nay"?

Forever, I know you'd love me.
Forever is what I need.
Forever, you want to give me.

But…

Forever seems like a dream.

NO MISTAKE

When it came to him, there was no *it wasn't supposed to happen*. Her emotions were heightened when it came to him, and she didn't want to stay away although she knew how.

She'd talk herself into coming back around.

She didn't accidentally stumble into his DMs or send that were supposed to be for someone else.

Ending up in his bed was no mistake.

TIME OF NEED

She stepped outside eager to breathe in fresh air,
overwhelmed from inhaling the bullshit being
exhaled into her direction.
Not smoke but lost hope.

Her heart wouldn't be able to handle the toxins.
The room was polluted with insecurity and doubts.
A pool of broken promises and shattered dreams
drowning in their negative thoughts of how life
should be, ignoring all attempts that led to safety.

Surrounded by lost souls,
questioning how her night brought her here.
Back in the place she left behind with people who
were a mirror of who she *used* to be.

Looking around, she knew she didn't belong.
In a place she no longer called home,
not one person she could call on
until he looked her way.

The only other person not hanging inside the
place.
His eyes immediately said, "Let me in, open up for
me."
Hesitant but intrigued by the story written on his
face sent her floating his way.

She could see him.
He could see her.

They no longer wondered why they gravitated toward a place filled with demons.

TEDDY

He was the last person I thought I'd vibe with.
He was always the first person in my corner…

HE WON'T

Turning his back on me is something he won't do
because his mama taught him how to love a lady
and how to remain true.

He doesn't treat me like his property; he knows he
doesn't own me, so if I decide to walk out the door,
he knows there's no stopping me.

But we'll never get to that chapter because he
knows we're together, and when I say, "It's a go,"
he's going to take his time pleasing every inch of
me, whenever and wherever.

TREASURE

He was her best kept secret, and she had no plans of revealing the man responsible for the permanent smile on her face.

She couldn't risk another trying to break in and steal what was hers…

FOR MY KING

I'm listening…

But do you hear what I'm saying?
Or do you let it go in one ear and out the other?

As your Queen, I'm here to make sure the moves
you make are logical and that every minor situation
doesn't end in devastation. All isn't meant to end in
war, especially when it comes to our love.

You have my back…

But I'm watching you from all angles.
No one is going to come through violating.

You correct my mistakes.
I right your wrongs.

I'm happy to be sharing this throne

CROSSING PATHS

I was still figuring out the ways of the world,
but I was happy to be on my journey with him.

He didn't put on a mask to disguise who he was.
He was flawed, a beautiful disaster just like me.
He was open; he let his thoughts flow like a river.

No matter how deep his thoughts went, he always
made sure everything that came out his mouth was
respectful, and I made sure I did the same.

He was ambitious; he didn't let anything stand in
his way, not even me.
He handled business, waited for me to handle
mine, and then we'd meet somewhere in-between.

We both had dreams, and we told ourselves we
wouldn't continue to sleep on what should be a
reality.

He wasn't just a dreamer but a believer.
He was motivated and oh so determined
He didn't have all answers, but he was willing to go
out there and get them.

He was on a journey of his own, traveling at 1000
mph, and he just so happened to find me on the
way to his destination.

LOVE WARS

When it called for it, I loved his aggression
The way he'd look at me with those crazy eyes
as he told me to "calm the fuck down."
Purposely, I'd continue with my attitude.
He'd approach me looking as if he was going to
strike.
Instead, he'd lift me by the waist, throw me on the
bed, and proceed to give me what I'd been craving
all day.

SOMETHING OLD, SOMETHING NEW

The week is coming to an end.
I've been looking forward to seeing you.
Remember the days I used to curve you?
The times I told you I found someone new,
someone worth missing out on you.

Now, I'd rather be with you
day-in and day-out spending time with you.
I promise you I don't want nobody new.

Baby, let me tell you, you the truth,
the realest man I've been next to.
I take pleasure in pleasing you.
So, tell me what you want me to do.

BLUE

Let's go deeper, beyond the surface.
I don't want to ride your wave.
I want to dive into you,
explore your ocean floor.

SMOOTH SAILING

She couldn't help but to pour herself into him.
She wasn't going to force the situation, but she
wasn't going to sabotage it either.
What they had was working.
She continued to let things flow.

It may have been silly to place all her eggs in one
basket, but if she proceeded with caution and
focused on the positive instead of worrying herself
with everything that could go wrong, it would all
work out in her favor.

Too often, she would jump to conclusions
The quickest way for things to go wrong is speaking
it into existence.

MORE THAN FRIENDS

I try not to overthink you because I'd hate to find out you don't feel the same way I do, but I think I could love you…

Don't know if I can say the same for you.

SHE'S HER EVERYTHING

She was a breath of fresh air. Her smile was a ray of sunshine on my darkest days. The sound of her voice when she spoke sounded like angels singing. Her hands felt like silk, and she smelled like the sweetest lavender.

I couldn't comprehend what I was feeling, but whenever she came around, I could feel fluttering in my stomach, and the drums beating in my chest. I wanted to brush off what I was feeling, but I couldn't ignore that, for the first time, I came across another human who spoke my love language.

She wasn't my best friend nor my lover but a soul I felt deeply connected to. Our energies intertwined bringing us to levels never reached.

Now, I know what people mean when they say, "love has no age, gender, or race." You can't put a label on something staring you dead in the face.

COFFEE

I crave the taste of you in the morning.
I can smell you from the other side of the room.
I anticipate having you home next to me daily.
You keep me up, especially those days I'm
exhausted.

You give me the energy I need to wake up in the
morning, put on my running shoes, and go chase
after everything I've predicted to come.

You keep me going when I feel like dropping
everything in front of me, turning around, and
running back to my bed.

You're there for me whenever I need you and for
the moments I don't.

I'm happy to have you here with me, Coffee.

CRYSTAL BALLS

I look into your eyes to get a glimpse of our future.
Curious to know if you see what I see.

AWAITING

Imagining all the great things to come.
Anticipating what I'll learn and come to cherish.
Envisioning the memories that will be made.
I visualize our chance at forever.
Us and the lives we create together.
That's why I don't give up on love.

GROWTH

Comes From Change

REVENGE ISN'T THE BEST MEDICINE

She used to be all about the get back…

You know, hurt him the way he hurt you.
Giving him a taste of his own medicine.
Playing phone tag and entertaining the next guy.
Lying in his face and creeping behind his back.
Going out with the guy she promised to stay far
away from.

She enjoyed playing the game until she didn't…

What was she getting out of messing with a few
guys that he knew? Not because she wanted to but
because she was confused.

Baby, you weren't hurting him; you were only
hurting you. Out in these streets looking like a fool
trying to do the things he does. Baby, he is not you.
Let him play the fool and you move on so you can
do you.

It's time to try something new.
Say "goodbye" for good this time.
Spend more time getting to know and love who
you are, so when he comes knocking at your door,
you'll be strong enough to say, "no more."

THE CHOICE IS YOURS

He placed his heart in the palm of my hand.
It took everything in me not to squeeze the life
from him.
This was his way of apologizing for all the damage
he had caused over the years.

He was placing his life in my hands, and as much
as I wanted to take it away from him, I couldn't
bring myself to instill that kind of pain upon him…

Sydney Reneé

THE BEGINNING OF THE END

I drove past his house for the fifth time today.
I couldn't bring myself to park the car.
I had every intention of knocking on his door.
I deserved to know why things were ending.
A *it's over* text couldn't erase our memories.

How could he possibly be over me?
Yesterday, he was on one knee begging to marry me.
Did hearing the word "No" cut him that deep?

It had nothing to do with me not loving him.
We just simply weren't ready to become a family.
We still hadn't worked through the issues existing.

Sure, I always dreamed of the day...

The day the man of my dreams got on one knee,
but this was different than what I imagined.
It was like he had to prove himself to somebody.
It was his way of telling the world he loved me
without every saying those words to me.

Looks like I'm walking into the beginning of our ending.

FAMILY AFFAIR

I could handle the lack of respect he showed me.
He'd been doing it for so long, it became routine.
I knew once I walked through the door, I'd be
getting cursed to hell by time we finished eating.
I figured, soon, I'd be dodging fists coming my
way.
I made my departure before we made it there.
I could handle the way I was being mistreated.
I couldn't handle my family being disrespected.

DANGEROUS

My heart wanted me to be with him,
but I continued to stay away.
Together, we weren't safe.

HOW YOU GONNA TELL ME?

It was easy for me to walk around giving my friends advice, but it wasn't easy for me to watch them ignore it.

How was I to tell them to walk away and never look back?

How was I going to tell them to stop picking up the phone and answering that knock at the door?

Where did I get off telling them what to do when it came to their relationships?

I never had any control of my own.

LIFE HAPPENS

Friends disappeared.
Lovers turned to enemies.
Betrayed by family.
These things changed her.
She started thinking differently.

BAD INTENTIONS

It didn't matter how kind she was.
It didn't matter how genuine she was.
People with bad intentions were always going to
take advantage of her.
She was starting to see that people got a kick out of
seeing how far they could push others.
If she kept allowing the bullshit, it was going to
continue to happen.

At some point, she had to put an end to it all.

WHAT ABOUT YOUR FRIENDS?

These days, I have no time to waste on what things could have or should have been. I don't have the time to give the ungrateful chance after chance. If you feel the need to question my loyalty, I feel it's appropriate for me to leave your ass in my past.

Friendships don't always last, nor are they meant to be a forever kind of thing.

Some people come into your life for a short, sometimes long period of time to teach you a lesson or two. Some good and some horrible, but they are much needed.

The good times you cherish. You try to hold on to them for as long as possible. The history you made together you assume is strong enough to keep the friendship going on for a few more years or even a lifetime.

Hopes of growing old together and being there for each other's happiest moments go out the window. You start to question if the friendship was ever real. How can someone you once told every secret to turn around and betray you? No longer am I looking at a friend but my closest enemy.

When they ask me, "What about your friends?" It's unfortunate that I have to say, "What about them?"

ME, MYSELF, AND I

They can't accept that it's you I've chosen.
"Of all the people in the world, why her?" they ask.
What does she have that we don't? they wonder.
"She has my best interest," I respond.
You all wanted to keep me below your level.
You guys couldn't handle my elevation.
I can't help that she meant more to me than you.
I had to choose myself for the sake of my sanity.

STAY WOKE

The problem was you, not me.
Saying I was sleeping on you, but you lived in a dream.
You couldn't see what was real, only what you wanted it to be.

FALLEN ANGEL

The Devil was standing in front of me,
gazing into my eyes, piercing deep into my soul,
making it impossible to turn away.

I was entrapped.

Looking through demonic eyes, I saw myself.
Roaming his world, I saw a replica of mine.
There, I began to realize I was no better than him.

Banished by those who saw me unfit.
Not accepting me for the person I had become.
Having thoughts unlike anyone else's.
Making me appear to be the rebellious one.

Misunderstood and judged just as he was.
Being looked down upon for all I've done.
My sins, he understood.
My mistakes, he made.
My pain, he felt.

He wasn't alone.
We were all fallen angels.
Earth was our home.
He just called his Hell.

SAFE & FAR AWAY

I had to accept the truth; he was always going to be someone I loved even if he wasn't the one, I was going to spend life with. We might not have been the best, but we were great. We loved each other hard but always on separate days. He'd let go, and I'd be holding on. When he came back around, the tables turned. This time, it would be me saying, "Goodbye. I can't do this anymore." We weren't perfect, but we knew the back and forth would never be worth it.

MARATHON

I fell back to see if he could catch up.
I got tired of running laps around him.
We were supposed to be in this race together, but
everyone in the stands could see I was in this alone.
I was going to cross the finish line, and he wasn't
going to be anywhere nearby.

It's funny how me chasing after him led to me
surpassing him.

FREQUENCIES

Until you take the time to understand,
my heart and my mind we'll never vibe.
You and I are not on the same wave.
You search for temporary.
I'm waiting on forever.

4 WORDS

All it took were four words to realize she should no
longer waste time. Almost three-years together, and
it never once crossed her mind.

"Are you in love?"
"Is this for life?"

I didn't want to say, "no," so the only thing I could
say was "I'm not sure." But I knew the answer, I
wasn't in love, and he wasn't the one who I'd be
building a life with.

It took those four words for her to realize that it
was time to say goodbye before wasting anymore of
his time.
I got involved with someone who knew what he
wanted out of life—a wife and a steady foundation.
She was still young, but when she couldn't come
out with a "Yes, I'm in love," she was sure it would
never happen.

THAT'S FINE

I could stand in front of you
pretending you still make my heart skip beats,
acting as if my feelings for you still exist.

...or I could turn around and go get my heart
because it already ran off with my soul.

You can watch me drift off in the distance,
knowing we won't be making our way back.
I'd be perfectly okay with that.

BOY, BYE!

You were in my face saying all the things I used to want to hear, diving deep into your soul that suddenly had this lovely glow. It was shining like I've never seen before. You had grown, but I had moved the fuck on.
So much time wasted…

I still had love for you, but at this point, it was fuck you. I just couldn't fuck with you knowing all the ignorant shit you do and disrespect you put me through. Everything had always been about you, and that's why I had to cut you off.

Now, here you are, in my face telling me everything I've always wanted to hear. Oh, it's funny how things change. All I could do was look you in the face and say, "Boy, get the fuck out of here!"

11:07 P.M.

I placed my phone on the nightstand.
I picked it up the minute he crossed my mind.
Maybe, I'd call and say goodnight.
I immediately changed my mind.
Why was he a thought when I wasn't?

BLOCKED

He was trying to get through, but she no longer wanted him to. They spent years jumping on and off the rollercoaster of love, but there was never any love between the two.

It was more of an ongoing soap opera, full of the extras and a ton of dramatics. He'd say, "sorry," she'd forgive him. Then, he'd be back on the same bullshit she thought they left behind, and she'd be right back in her feelings.

She was growing tired, and it was only so much time that would pass before they were back on the same 'ol shit. She would tell him to stop calling, and, for a while, he would. She knew she was great at ignoring him, but she also knew, eventually, she'd give in.

It was time for them to cut all ties. She deleted the text thread, the call log, his name out of her contacts list., and then added his number to the block list. There was no way he was getting through, and she couldn't reach out even if she wanted to.

It was time to stop allowing the disrespect and negative energy into her life. All that shit needed to be blocked, and he was the first on her list.

THAT'S NOT MY JOB

It's not on me to make you feel like you're a
priority in my life when you're absent in mine.
It's not my job to make sure you are happy with
everything going on around you.

I shouldn't have to go out my way to please a
person who shows no interest in me or my well-
being. I shouldn't have to check in on a person who
can't make room in their day to see if I'm doing
fine.

It's not my job to do shit period. Treat people how
you want to be treated, and it might be
reciprocated.

THE PERFECT VACATION

She was looking for an escape in him when all
along she needed to look within herself.
There, she would have found the paradise she was
yearning for.

BLANK SPACE

She laid in bed staring out her window.
It was around 1 p.m., and the skies were gray.
There were no clouds resting above.
There wasn't a bird or plane in sight.
The sky was as empty as her heart,
but she wasn't in a dark place.
She wasn't hurting over her past.
She didn't hate who she was.
All the negative feelings she had washed away.
Honestly, she hadn't felt anything for a long time.
For her sanity, it was best to let all emotions fade.
She felt safer living that way.

ANGEL

She wanted him to be great…
But her approach didn't always come off as her
being loving and supportive. He sees it as her being
a bitch, always on his case. She wasn't going to sit
around watching him go to waste. She pushed him
until he got off his ass.

She lost him during the process.

But he could never say she wasn't a blessing sent
his way.

LETTER TO MY EX

Letting go of you was the hardest story I've ever had to tell, but truth be told, it was a story that should have never begun.

You weren't supposed to be a main character. You weren't even supposed to have a damn chapter, and even when we came to an end, our saga was one that couldn't be discontinued.

I've thought about burning every book with the story of us two, but then I'd have to burn right along with them because every second of every minute we spent together is engraved in the back of my head and the part of my heart that still beats for you.

Maybe, I could tear up all the pages that included the good times we shared only to leave me with the moments you ripped out my heart and I continuously stabbed you in the chest. But then I'd be stuck remembering the times you picked it back up and gently placed it back in my chest as I tended to the wounds on yours.

No matter how I try to erase you, I'll be left trying to convince myself I hate you a little more than I love you.

AT PEACE

It felt good being free, away from you and the hell you had me living through. Surrounded by your demons and the scorching flames that left marks on my face. Cuts on my wrist and ankles from the countless times I tried to break away. Someone had to be watching me from the highest. Watching as I fought a battle that was impossible to win, but the possible happened I broke free and flew far away.

...finally, at peace.

ME vs. ME

I never understood people who said their biggest
battle was the one with themselves.

It wasn't until I came face-to-face with the side of
me, I disliked.

It was me against the disbeliefs I faced, and I was
coming in last place.
Doubt takes over, then anxiety kicks in, leaving me
stuck.
Watching the Devil on one shoulder and an Angel
on the other battle it out.
The Universe worked hard to show me the way
out.
I always went in the opposite direction.

The side of me that was fearless did all she could to
help me out.

BEAUTIFUL

Looking in the mirror, watching flashbacks of the
girl she formerly was.

There was a lot about her she didn't love.

She now welcomes the tiger strips; love handles
and extra fluff around her midsection.
The extra meat and dimples that are now her
thighs.

What she once thought was ugly, she found beauty
in.

SUNNY DAYS

There was a dark cloud following me.
Everywhere I went, it tagged along like a best friend.
Every now and then, the sun would come shining through, letting me know everything would come together again.

HOURS

Driving down the freeway, she smiled while taking
in the beauty of the place she called home.
The sun partially blinded her as she sang along to
every song.

She began to think about her life and was filling up
with joy, but at the same time she was overcome
with fear.

SATURDAY NIGHT FEELS

I want to be able to open myself up in ways I've
never imagined. To walk in my truth and swim
freely in my emotions without judgement.
I want to fall madly in love with my flaws and let
no one come between us. To look at all things
through positive eyes even when it doesn't rub me
right.
I want to love another unconditionally, accepting
him for all he is, for all he used to be, and for all he
will become.
I want to keep my mind strong and remain happy.

HIS KEEPER

Restless days and sleepless nights.
Exhausted, as if I hadn't slept one day in my life.
Pushing through the days was nothing nice.
It was then that I knew I had formed a life.

Within two seconds, there they were—two pink
lines.

Shocked? Absolutely not.
I asked to be blessed in this way.
Sooner than expected but expected.

From that day on, I knew I loved you.
I was going to do everything in my power to keep
you out of harm's way.

My duty *was* and will always be to protect you.

Before you had a heartbeat, I was afraid I was
going to lose you.

In my apartment alone, looking down at the blood
on the tissue.

For a second there, I thought I lost you.

Gone, missing out on life before you had a chance
to show the world who you are.

I prayed long and hard that night as I went
through all this alone but finding out you were
okay brought so much peace to our home.
It was in that moment I knew I loved you more
than myself.

SEED

As the seasons passed, I watched you grow.
Finally, I understood what it meant to feel alive.
Whenever I felt butterflies, it was you saying, "hi."
For months, I watched as you rested on my side.
Though painful, I was happy you were keeping me
aware you were alive.
You blossomed into the most beautiful being I'd
ever seen.

Born with a crown, you're for sure a King to be.

MOTHERHOOD

The moment I became a mother, life changed.
I knew I'd have to be stronger than what I was.
I had to become selfless because I was no longer
alone. There wasn't a book that could prepare me
for what was to come. After all, not every
experience was the same. Either, I had it or I
didn't, and let me tell you…

Baby, I was made for this shit

NOTES FROM SHE

I leave you with these words

TOGETHER, WE COULD WIN

I applaud the woman who sees the good in other women.
The woman who doesn't see competition when looking into the eyes of another. Instead, she sees a friend, a business partner, someone she can create and have healthy conversation with.

The woman who smiles and gives you a friendly "hello" when you walk by instead of shooting daggers your way.

More women need to learn how to work with each other and be supportive of one another instead of creating problems that don't exist.

SHOWSTOPPER

Dear, Queen,

It's hard to go unnoticed in a room full of fakes and phonies…you are rare.

Love,
SHE

EMPOWERED, WE ARE

To my Queens:

I love how as women we can bounce back from the shit going on in our lives as if nothing ever happened. We work through our feelings in a matter of seconds, and then get back to the regular scheduled program. Before we walk out the house, we dry our eyes, put a smile on, and take on the world like the superwomen we are. That's strength right there.

Sincerely,
SHE

YOU SHOULD KNOW

To Whom It May Concern:

If they have no problem wasting your time, they shouldn't make it an issue when you move the fuck on with your life.

Sincerely,
SHE

SWEET SAVAGE

To Whom It May Concern:

When you're a good person, you tend to get fucked over. It's just the reality of the world we live in unfortunately. People see someone they think they can take advantage of, and they love to see how far they can push you. They forget that not everyone is going to stick around and take their shit. Guess what? You've suddenly turned into the evil villain because you had to go savage and let them know, "You got the wrong bitch."

Sincerely,
SHE

A MESSAGE ON FRIENDSHIP

Stop pretending like you want to rebuild friendships when you come face-to-face with an old friend. If those aren't your intentions, please don't be fake; keep your eyes to the ground, mouth closed, and feet moving. There's no point in starting up a conversation that you have no plans on continuing.

DOWNFALL

Sometimes, you must talk yourself off the fucking ledge because the person directly next to you, the one who is supposed to have your best interest at heart, is the one praying you take that plunge.

NOTE TO SHE

Giving up on your hopes and dreams is giving up
on yourself while letting down all those who believe
in you.
It would have been easy to walk away and settle for
a life you know you don't want.

Walking away from your dreams would be the
beginning of the unhappy life you'd be living, but,
this time, you wouldn't be able to escape the
reality.

Working jobs, you don't want with people you
can't stand. Struggling to get out of bed so you and
your child can eat and have clothes on your backs.
Counting down the days till the weekend came,
yelling, "Freedom" as soon as you walk out of the
office.

Giving up on your dreams aren't a part of your
destiny. Time to stop doubting the talent God
bestowed upon you.

THE REAL MVPs

To Whom It May Concern:

Start surrounding yourself with people who want to see you win in life, those people who aren't afraid to speak up when you're in the wrong. Keep around those who give you constructive feedback even if it could possibly hurt your feelings. That's not their intention. They truly want you to succeed. Surround yourself with people who believe in you even in times you don't believe in yourself. Eliminate those toxic relationships in your life and focus on the genuine ones you do have.

Sincerely,
SHE

SOMETHING TO THINK ABOUT

Dear, Queens and Kings,

They may make you happy now, but never place your happiness in another person's hands. There may be a point in time when things change. Then who are you going to turn to for the joy you once felt? Are you just going to cling to someone new?

Sincerely,
SHE

FOR MY LOVERS

My Kings and Queens,

Be with someone you can laugh with, be goofy as fuck with, and the sound of happiness coming from your mouth puts an immediate smile on their face. Someone you can open every part of yourself up to even the parts you hide from those closest to you. Someone who makes you feel safe no matter the place. A person you can have disagreements with, but you both can come to an understanding and are never too prideful to admit when either of you are in the wrong. A person who brings out the best in you and pushes you every day to be better than you were the day before. A person you can see a forever with even when forever officially comes to an end. You know you'll see each other in the next lifetime to start your new journey.

Sincerely,
SHE

STICKY NOTES ON HER MIRROR

Queen,

When you know your worth, you know what you deserve, and no one can tell you different.
Once you know who you are, once you've come to love yourself and realize how valuable you are, you'll stop lowering your standards and letting people talk you into believing you can't do any better.

You have control!

Sincerely,
SHE

STICKY NOTES ON HER MIRROR

Dear, Queen,

When you feel down because he made you feel like nobody, go look in the mirror and remind yourself you're the one, the two, and the three.

You are *everything*!

Sincerely,
SHE

NOTES ON HER WINDOW

Queen,

Don't let a man be the reason you stop chasing
your dreams…remember, you're more than a
trophy on his shelf.

Love,
Yourself

HEY, LADIES

Queens,

I admire women who speak up for themselves and for what's right because I used to be a woman who didn't know how to. It takes a lot of courage to put your opinions out into the universe and deal with the negativity thrown back your way. I used to be afraid of the reactions I would possibly receive. You ladies are an inspiration.

Yours truly,
SHE

NOTES ON HER MIRROR

Dear, Queen,

Grind until you reach your goal.
Then, proceed to grind some more.

Sincerely,
SHE

LETTERS ON HER DRESSER

My Beloved,

You must be willing to take risks
as well as handle rejection.
It's okay to be pushed a few steps back but
never stop moving forward.
Push your way through every obstacle.
Don't stop what's meant for you.
Success is on the other end.

Sincerely,
The One Who Almost Let Go

A MESSAGE FOR MY KINGS

To My Handsome Fellas,

Believe in her like she believes in you.
King, she's got dreams that she's making come true.

Sincerely,
SHE

BEFORE I GO

Remember, there will always be someone out there who doesn't agree with the things you do and/or like the person you decide to spend your life with. Everyone can't understand the choices we make, and it's not for them to. If what you're doing makes you happy, keep doing it. If you're with someone you connect with on more levels than one, can laugh and smile with, who makes you want to be better, who feels like home and more, don't let another's opinion make you walk away. These people aren't you; they have no clue what's right or wrong when it comes to you.